HIPPIE SPEEDBALL

Hippie Speedball

Ly Faulk

Querencia Press – Chicago IL

QUERENCIA PRESS

© Copyright 2025
Ly Faulk

ISBN 978 1 963943 87 0

www.querenciapress.com

First Published in 2025

Querencia Press, LLC
Chicago IL

Printed & Bound in the United States of America

contents

Putting The Lake Behind My Grandmother's House To Bed

The lake behind my grandmother's house misses me.
It says that children no longer play
In its murky waters. It misses
1991, the year my cousins came to stay
for the summer. We grew pink under
the Georgia sun, collecting tadpoles
and swimming for hours. The lake
behind my grandmother's house misses the tadpoles too.
It sighs and admits that it has dried up over the years.
Perhaps it isn't the lake it once was. But
that shouldn't mean that it gets left behind.

I nod and agree with the lake. In a perfect world,
I would drive the four hours to the house
where my grandmother used to live. I would
shed my city skin and wrap the humid swamp air
around me. My hair would frizz again and
my limbs would grow shorter. I would toddle
down the dirt path, and dip my toes into the
cool, welcoming water that misses me so much.
I may never see that lake again, so
I blow it a kiss, tell it a bedtime story,
and sneak out the backdoor as it sleeps.

Spring Offering

I chew grass,
blades caught in my teeth,
green juice running down my chin.
I crawl on all fours,
naked in the chilly spring air.
Shoveling handfuls of dirt into my mouth,
I devour loam, pebbles, worms,
moss, grasshoppers, mice.
I peel off my skin
and dance about,
just muscle and bone.
I strip off the muscle until I am
but a chattering skeleton on the
verdant field of spring.
I offer my bones to the wind and become
dust.

Still Life But Make It Autobiographical

I have kept this plant alive for   three years and some months.

this is a record for me.

I have kept this body alive for   41 years and   5 months.

this is also a record.

She shrivels in on herself   this plant   when she needs.

She signals me with dry soil and   for once I'm sensitive to the signs.

[so many shriveled   black leaves came before.]

Brown leaves   cling   to her vines but she perseveres.

green greets me every morning.

She breathes out as   I   breathe in.

I think about lowering the blinds.

letting her wither   away.

I think about letting the dry soil   strangle   her roots until

she is not my   responsibility

But I keep the blinds open   and

green greets me

Another morning.

Would You Still Love Me?

Would you still love me if I was a worm? If I ate dirt and couldn't speak and everyone thought of you as the weirdo with the worm fetish? Would your heart still skip a beat if I slithered by? Would you build me a tiny worm house with a worm bed for me to sleep on? Would you find the finest soils for me to eat? What if I were chopped in half and grew into two worms? Would you love us both? Are you still awake?

Middle-Aged Mermaid

Soft skin that has more give than it used to; always from a place of giving; I give more than I used to; some say used up but my fins still glimmer in the filtered sunlight; my eyes still glimmer when I speak your name; sunlight shines through my skin; translucent from too long in the dark; my voice cracks from overuse; I'm always talking, laughing, smoking, crying; I've sold my voice too many times for land legs; it comes back a little more broken each time; I come back to you a little more broken each time; I give more of myself each time I break a little more broken each time; as the waves break over me, foam resurrecting me; I know now that the sea is my true love; resurrecting and reclaiming me; I am home.

Burning, I Rise

There's no poetry in this pain,
only stinking piles of laundry that go unwashed,
dirty dishes caked with last night's dinner,
roaches that keep coming back
no matter how many times you kill them,
binge-watching shows you know by heart
as the clock keeps
tick tick ticking away the days.

The days stack one after another
like boxes to be checked off.
I cling to my bed, to the lightness of sleep,
the weightless void of dreams.
It is empty and it aches. However,
burning, I rise. Like smoke toward
the heavens, I rise. With hope on
my lips and tangles in my hair,

I rise.

Those Moments of Gender Euphoria

Against a bright blue sky, I become myself.
I fly against azure field,
wind whipping around me, kissing my skin.
Birds visit and fly near me and we
sing songs to each other under the bright sun.

My body unfurls.
Relaxed, at last, I own me,
I wave like a flag.

Metamorph

My head is wrapped in clouds,
stony-eyed, and skin striped
in bisexual and trans color schemes.
I move like a drunk cat:
thrown off balance
by my bitch tits and tiny feet.
I get "ma'am"ed in public.
It rolls off of me and I wonder
who they're talking to.
I don't gender like they do.
I don't queer like you do either.
I'm a secret third thing.
I am Schrodinger's gender
so when you kiss me,
you are Schrodinger's gay.
I spread my secret third thing for you
and tell you to touch gently.

Benediction

My grandma carries me to Sunday School at 10 AM on the dot. Later, her liver-spotted hands wrap around the navel oranges that she peels just for the two of us, onion paper-thin skin cracking open in places, letting the juice in. Orange slices in a tin pan and the smell of citrus heavy in the air. I fall asleep and she carries me to threadbare sheets and flat pillows. Kisses curly head and hums a dreamful tune. 8 years dead but she is not gone. Grandma carries me, oh how she carries me.

Still, she carries me.

Unemployment Bingo

B	I	N	G	O
I am putting ambition's feet up and mixing it a drink.	So it's problematic the way that I fall in love with hunger pangs.	I linger on the dark intrusive thoughts that litter my mind,	like the great garbage islands in the oceans.	And what of all the dead bodies that litter the sides of Everest?
Didn't they once sit at ambition's feet like a beloved golden retriever?	Me, I wear pajamas at an expert level.	I nap at Olympic standards.	Coffee flows like poetry through sticky fingers.	I am putting my feet up and smoking another bowl.
I call it a hippy speedball, a little bit up, a little bit down.	I scrape the bottom of the barrel looking for a feeling to have.	★	Life passes over me like sand.	My fingers are numb and the edges are too smooth.
I move with a certain haze these days.	Singular poetics, divorced from context.	I have purple hair and visible tattoos,	I can't pass a drug test and I always show up smelling loud.	No grind for the culture. No culture in the grind.
Is there such a thing as commuter trauma?	Traffic chokes the town like a jawbreaker lodged in a throat.	Mother, I crave poetry!	There's no money in poetry, she said and laughed in my face.	These self-destructive seizures will end me.

Dead Air

They say the static
of a dead channel
is the cold rattling
of a dead star,
spending its last moments
begging
to be heard one last time.

Nebulas Touching In The Dark

—After Falling Star

you pierce me through with divine ecstasy

mixing your star stuff with my star stuff, we

explode and dissolve into a sea of

pearls, floating in the in-between when you

promised that we would be remembered by

literary historians and the

astronomers alike. forming our own

constellations across the black heavens

falling like meteors, streaking across

velvet backgrounds and ethereal planes.

the beauty of the night sky makes us weep

fat tears because our fate is not written

in their mysteries but rather in our

grey stellar dust and blue whispered secrets.

Overboard

sweet stockholm syndrome beats like a hammer
the false anniversaries calling us to worship at the sea where
waves splash in unison with lovers making love;
unruly boys covered in calamine thrashing throughout
the house with plates glued to fingers, bringing the hose
into the house and spraying the manipulator love hero
directly in his dreamy face

the twice-named woman reveals the deception and
makes away with her riches. wonders of the world
rot in the rain as masculine joy withers in the absence
of feminine labor

she descends, sweeping them all out to sea with her wing
around their necks,
holding them close to her crimson-beating breast.

Time Lord

I swallow a broken clock, chewing gears and the minute hand between my yellow teeth. The alarm bells go down hard. The second hand goes down soft. You ask me for the time, stalling; I tell you it's too late. I already ate the time and now time stands still. The next words never leave your mouth and you stay with me here in this suspended moment where the light refracts in the lens of your glasses and the glare makes me squint and I never love someone so much as when they are leaving me.

Literary Dreams

I want to write about sweaty thighs and cheap typewriters,
whiskey and swans,
The moon and everyone in love with the moon.
I am in love with the moon and I wouldn't have it any other way.
I want my whiskey on the rocks and my swans singing songs
about how this is the end of them.
I want to write about abandoned little girls and broken hearts.
The abandoned little girls would have a redemption arc and
there would be a silver lining to the heartbreak stories.
I want to write about ordinary heroes and extraordinary villains.
The villains will be irresistible
the heroes will be dads or something.
I like stories with dads—I know this says something about me.
I want to write about happy endings and love found and kept.
I want a happy ending

I Don't Want To Be A Person Anymore

I'm a little hedgehog,
writing my little
hedgehog poems.
I'm binding them into a book,
written on onion skin
with ground-up indigo
as ink.

On Surviving For Another Year

July was all sweat and red cheeks. The hot air stifled all ambition and reduced me to a mewling kitten. I curled into myself, drifting through fitful sleeps and sleepy awakenings. I rotated in bed like a rotisserie chicken. The labor of staying alive. Setting dates like breadcrumbs. *I have to stay alive until Labor Day. I have to stay alive until the first day of fall. I have to stay alive ...*

December was all a blur. Unseasonably warm. There will be more winter days in t-shirts according to the news. Christmas in shorts. I count back to how many winters it has been since the institution. I count the hours until the new year rolls over. I set my dates like breadcrumbs. *I have to stay alive until my poem is published. I have to stay alive until Valentine's Day. I have to stay alive ...*

Mushroom Wave

weaving in and out of traffic
narrowly missing rear-ending a minivan and
almost sideswiping a motorcycle
you must get to the bean burrito
you're so hungry and it's going to save your life
like it always has
add sourcream during the vegetarian days
no cheese during the vegan days
nowadays you just take it how it comes
the sky is a gold pale blush and
you've got the top down breathing in
the spring flowers and exhaust like you're never gonna die
not if you get this burrito you're going to live fucking forever
and
it's not just the drugs talking
you've got this
the vinyl seat sticks to your thighs and
the air conditioner is broken its blasting heat
in mid-summer and you don't have the dough
to fix it but that life-saving, dawn-bringing burrito
is only 99 cents.

Cancer is a Crab

Clattering clawing thing,
scattering away from embrace

and whispering tongues.
Aptly named, Cancer grows

silently along your spine
insinuating while remaining

armored. They will ride for you,
die for you, but they won't

crack open their shell for you.
You will burn for them,

yearn for them, but they are too
in love with the moon,

waiving pincers like knives, threatening
to cut open the clear night sky.

Be Nice To Your Cremation Technician

Bathe your body with excellent fatty foods so that you burn more quickly. Go soft in the joints and hard places. Your cremation technician can only burn so many bodies in a day so be sure to light up like a candle inside the oven. Be blue flame curling up towards the heavens. Refrain from excreting too many gases on your way out. Be flammable, but not too explosive. A steady flame for your cremation technician to lose themselves in, staring at the dancing heat until it dwindles. Be smoldering coals with chunks of the person you used to be. Do not fight against the dying of the flame. Your cremation technician has other bodies to burn.

Thin Lines

I am a house on fire, a pillar of   smoke trailing toward heaven, a black cloud hanging over your head, white noise as you   sleep, wallpaper peeling up around the edges, a seedling bursting through the dirt, a secret   hidden in the files, the search engine that spills the beans that clack on the countertop, the   thin lines of cocaine that I can already taste in the back of my throat, the intoxication of   bitterness that keeps you up at night, a crack of lightning in the dark of the storm, a raven   squawking for more trinkets, clawing at the dirt.

Acknowledgments

☺ "Those Moments of Gender Euphoria" was previously published by *Corporeal*

☺ "Metamorph" was previously published by *Fifth Wheel Press*

☺ "Unemployment Bingo" was previously published by *Bullshit Lit*

☺ "Dead Air" & "I Don't Want To Be a Person Anymore" were previously published by *Tiny Wren Lit*

☺ "Be Nice to Your Cremation Technician" & "Thin Lines" were previously published by *Roi Feineant*